Ladies – You're welcome. Fellas – Sorry!
© 2021 Dominic Chase

ISBN 978-1-09839-239-0

eBook ISBN 978-1-09839-240-6

LADIES – YOU'RE WELCOME.

FELLAS –
Sorry!

DOMINIC CHASE

CONTENTS

PREFACE

Hello Ladies! First off, thank you very, very much for purchasing this book – it is truly appreciated from the bottom of my warm-hearted cold heart ☺. Let me start off my stating what my objective is here. The goal of this book is to enlighten you ladies on the many tricks, trades, and general pattern recognition of us men. The purpose of this book, is to help you navigate through the BS that we feed you on a daily basis!

Now I realize you all are smart, in fact, you all are way smarter than us. But I notice that when it comes to your significant other, that you tend to overlook certain things, either because you are truly unaware or because you do so knowingly and are willing to accept it. In my years of personal experience, research, and extensive discussions about these topics, about 80% of men have something to hide. So hopefully this book puts you in a position to identify these habits, discover the truth, and help you make an informed decision about what to do next. Again, frankly speaking, 8 out of 10 men have some type of dirt on their shoes. It's up to you that when you find it, you either give him the chance to clean them up or you decide to just throw them out and get a new pair.

Secondly, I do apologize for my tone at times throughout the book. All of the anecdotes and stories within the book are 100% true so I tend to use crass/expletive language quite a bit as I am excerpting real situations and exerting my frustrations. I truly am not trying to be demeaning at all, I just want to be as real as possible and give you my perspective, to ultimately help you.

Fellas – As you can probably already tell, if you are a bad dude when it comes to women, then yeah, I'm sorry for doing this. But, if you happen to be one of the rare good ones out there, then you'll thank me......you'll see...

WHY IS STEVE FROM WORK CALLING YOU AT 2:00 A.M.?

Ladies, you see that we only have one phone, and every time a text or call comes in it is either a guy or our mom and dad. So, everything must be cool and you have the perfect man, right? Unfortunately, it is not likely. Here are a couple of things to investigate ... I am sorry fellas... again.

GHOST PHONE PROTOCOL

There are several ways for men to do this, but here is the primary means I am aware of. There is this app called g-voice, or Google Voice. It is basically a way to have a second phone number, but using the same phone. So you will never find a second "ghost" phone that we use for bad things, unfortunately we have become a little smarter in this regard. If only we could use our smarts to do good in life, right?!?!

Using Google voice, we can text and call as if we are using a second, completely different phone with a brand-new number. We can even choose what number we want. For example, in case we meet a girl while in New York City at a club, we can say we live in New Jersey to throw you off, or even say we are from Miami with a 305 area code to be cooler and also to have the notion that we are from out of town. I know what you are thinking, and yes, we ARE that low.

So, what you need to do is get a hold of his phone and swipe through all of the pages and go through each app on his phone. If you see the g-voice app, you have a problem and know the type of man you really are dealing with. Call him out and see what he has to say. If he's smooth, he will make up something good, but know that it is pure garbage.

- Their likely response: "Oh babe, I use that for work. They assigned me a second number."

  · Your proposed response: "No, they didn't. There is a Good or Blackberry Work app that is used for this purpose."

- Their likely response: "I have no idea what that is, it downloaded automatically with the new software."

  · Your proposed response: "Nothing downloads automatically, sorry."

- Their likely response: "I use this to call internationally to my cousin sweetie."

  · Your proposed response: "Nope, WhatsApp is used for that."

Or the classic…they will try to turn this situation around by getting mad at you about no trust in the relationship, which will likely also divert your attention from the matter at hand, so beware of this move. It will likely go something like this….

Their likely response: "I have no idea what this app is, maybe it downloaded through a software update with one of my other apps... Don't you trust me?!"

Your proposed response: "Okay, cool, no problem, I hear what you are saying. So let's open it up together right now and then I won't ever bring it up again."

Pretty reasonable ask I'd say. But sadly, he won't. He will throw out another excuse not to open it up, or he will storm out and leave, or suddenly go to the bathroom to delete the evidence.

WHATSAPP

WhatsApp is great, right? You can call friends and family internationally for free. You can set up several different group chats. You can also see if your message was delivered and even when they actually read it. Fantastic functionality, I know!

But there is a key feature on WhatsApp that people either don't know about or they don't think twice about. You can essentially turn all notifications from WhatsApp off. This includes calls, texts, and read receipts. If all notifications are off, you will never see a WhatsApp notification popup. So this means that guys can easily use this feature to talk to a woman, and hide the entire notification aspect of it. But when they open up the phone [in private], everything will appear as if from thin air. And on the other end, WhatsApp calls and texts go through like normal. They never go straight to voicemail so it doesn't look odd to the woman on the side.

So – because of this nifty feature, another red flag to consider is when a guy gets your number and contacts you via WhatsApp instead of text. If he does this, question him on it casually. See what he says and check it on your BS radar.

"Oh, WhatsApp is easier" – doubtful. If he is persistent about using it, turn it off for a little bit and say your phone needs an update to use WhatsApp, but the update keeps giving you an error. Tell him you are going to Verizon to check it out, but for now he should just text. See what happens, as it's pretty hard to dance around that one.

Unless on date number four, he drives by a Verizon store on purpose and says, "Oh, hey, why don't we get your phone fixed, the movie doesn't start for an hour." Please don't mistake this for kindness, ladies, he's not just trying to help you fix your phone out of the kindness of his heart. Anything we do is usually for our own benefit. So, ladies, if he goes to the extreme lengths to do this:

- He is smooth as fuck, and you are dealing with a true professional.

- Just leave him, because if he is capable of something like this, there's plenty more he will do to keep you around on the side. Trust me, you are better off in the long run. This dude is a pro and will break your heart.

Pure and simple, text messaging is the easiest way to contact someone. It is also the hardest to hide. You cannot easily turn text notifications off. You can block a person from texting you completely, but guys won't normally do this because you will know when they do (the blue bubble will turn green when you text him), and it will become instantly shady. So ladies, push the text agenda, and stay away from WhatsApp for day-to-day contact, and use it sparingly, as needed!!!

MODIFY CONTACT

This is also a crafty little trick we men use to, unfortunately, do bad things to women. Because when you see that Steve from work is texting throughout the day, all is well right? Probably not. Guys don't communicate THAT much, and if they do then there may be an entirely different type of problem on your hands.

You can do a few things in this scenario. Start paying a little closer attention for one. Know that we are slick, and we have ways to smoothly check things. We turn around for a second to check who that text was from, and then slip it right back into the pocket if it's another beau. We go refill our drink in the kitchen and use the fridge door as a shield to cover ourselves and check. We head to the bathroom to "wash our hands" for no reason. If we're really good (or bad rather), we just run the water so it sounds like we are washing, but really we are on our phones. We take trips to the bedroom for no apparent reason. So if you start seeing these patterns, you should know that something is probably up.

Also, start physically hanging out closer to your man, and pay attention for the vibration noise. Because you know full and well, that phone will most likely be on silent while you guys are hanging out. So when he gets up to go to the kitchen, say you are hungry too and jump up with him. See how he reacts when you say, "babe, I think your phone just went off." If he takes it out right away and looks at the screen in front of you, you have a good man on your hands. But he won't. He will say, "okay, cool" and then kind of "forget" about it until you do. But that will be the only thing on his mind until he can check it, so he will likely get up again in a minute for some other bullshit reason.

Also, here is an insider tip. After we get comfy with you girls and start seeing your patterns, we get lazy! So, if a text comes in, we sometimes may just read it close by you because we think you are too stupid to realize what we are doing (I know that was harsh). Pay attention for these key opportunities ladies and watch from the corner of your eye and read that damn message. If you see a picture of a girl or a flirty emoji, call him out on it right away. Don't wait for another time.

But here is what it boils down to. If he is too good and you can't capitalize on the above, just look for who's sending him a message or calling. If he's overly confident, he will leave his phone out in front of you so you can see also, and that reassures you in two ways.

1. It makes you think, *oh well he's a good guy because his phone is out right where I can see it*

2. *Oh it's just Steve from the office, not a girl.*

But no, more likely than not it's not Steve from the office, it's Lisa instead. So, if Steve is texting all the time and calling, like I said you may have another problem on your hands if it is actually Steve. But odds are it is Lisa, and he modified the name in his phone and he is sleeping with her or trying to.

So call him out. If you get up to use the restroom while you both are sleeping, tap his phone screen and see what's going on. If you see there is a call from Steve at 11 p.m. or 2 a.m., then you know something is up. Guys don't call or text other guys like that, but women do. Especially if they are drinking and they start missing you, they will call or text. Wake him up and ask, "Why is Steve calling you so late? Let's see what his text message says, maybe he needs you."

If he checks in front of you, awesome!! But if he says, "Ahh, it's all good. He's probably just out and wants me to stop by for a drink," and puts his phone down without checking, but then gets up in five minutes to go to the bathroom and takes his phone with him, you're in trouble, baby.

We do this with multiple people, too. Oftentimes we use the names of former co-workers so it's tough for you to verify the validity of the person from your end. There are names he has probably mentioned two or three times total, so it's not so far-fetched to see them texting him. But he's not talking to a guy, it's a woman. So call him out on it when you suspect it, make him show you the text message trail with Steve to see if it really is, in fact, Steve.

IS YOUR PHONE GLUED INSIDE YOUR POCKET?

This is a dead giveaway, ladies. If you never see a guy's phone when you are hanging out, there's major concern.

If it is inside his pocket the entire time you guys are hanging out, it's a problem. If he leaves his phone in his car, it's a bigger problem.

Do a quick test, just to see what happens. When you are at dinner, ask him to show you a picture of something random, maybe a recent picture of a pet or a sibling. Observe his reaction at all stages. When you ask him, does he hand you the phone? If your boo gets up and comes to your side of the booth to show you a picture and then gets up and goes back to his side after the picture showing is over, he is cheating for sure. But the really slick ones will usually just show you their phone from their arm, not letting you even touch the phone. The slickest and truest players will give you their phone, because they have gone through and deleted the evidence right before your date, and they will act like they aren't even flinching when you have their phone.

But pay particular attention to what he does after. Does he put the phone back in his pocket? If so, that's a flag. If he leaves it out on the table, is it face down? That's a flag. If he leaves it face up, this could be a good sign, but again it could not. Because as other sections of the book have alluded to, he can change contact names or block certain people for a little bit during dinner. Then you are dealing with a true connoisseur of the game. To crack this guy, you'll need to throw the Hail Mary, as mentioned in the last section of the book.

WHAT WOMEN REALLY WANT

Ladies, why do you tell your man to always tell the truth when it is the exact opposite you want in reality? I mean, you are practically begging us to lie to you. It boggles my mind!

LIE TO ME, PLEASE!

Before I got married, I had a decent rotation going on. It was fun, I had six women (give or take) that I would go out with, chill, you know … all that great stuff. A few of them were cool, they understood the situation and didn't ask questions. I am assuming they were doing their own thing also, which was a-okay with me. But a few of them kept yapping about the fact that we should be honest with each other. I kept hearing, "No matter what, let's just be honest. Even if it will hurt…"

So after a few months of ignoring that and just continuing down the path of rotation, I was out with one of the virtuous ones, felt bad, and said *fuck it – why not*? I was bored and thought, *Let's switch things up and tell the truth*. So I was out one night with this particular woman, we went to dinner and were heading home. She brought up the fact that

I didn't reply to some bullshit text the night before. Usually I would just lie and say I was asleep or didn't hear my phone, but since she regularly brought up the fact that we should be honest no matter what I said fuck it. [Disclaimer: She was on the lower end of the rotation just so you know, so maybe that egged the situation on further also, because I didn't really give a fuck if she left me.]

So while I drove I respond by saying, "Actually I was with another girl last night and was occupied."

I could feel her looking at me, "Oh really!? Who were you with and what were you doing?"

I was thinking, *Come on number six, just shut the fuck and accept the role you know you are playing here.* But I wasn't mean enough to be that honest, and instead I decided to just set myself free and tell the whole truth this time. I then proceeded to say, "I was with Jennifer and we were either having dinner, watching a movie, or having sex, I can't remember exactly what time you texted me." Then it was on—World War III—she started crying, yelling, throwing shit, you name it. Here is how the next series of questions and events played out, and again, I decided to just stick to my guns this time and tell the plain truth in each of my responses:

- Her: "Why would you tell me this right now?"

  · Me: "You said to be honest no matter what."

- Her: "How could you do this to me?"

  · Me: "I told you from the start that I did not want a relationship with you and that I was seeing other women."

- Her: "You never told me about other women!"

- Me: "Yes I did. I clearly said so from the get go and also told you a few times over the course of this thing. It seems like you just kind of mentally blocked it out."

- Her: "So now what do you want?"

  - Me: "Well apparently I did not do a good job of explaining how this would work, so I'm sorry for that, but I am going to continue seeing other women. It looks like that has upset you, so what would you like to do?"

- Her: "Yeah, we are done, go fuck yourself!"

  - Me: "Cool, thanks. Goodbye."

- [Less than twenty-four hours later] Her: "Sorry about last night, want to come by?"

  - Me: "Be over in about an hour or so, I'm at Jen's."

    - Her: "Okay."

So after all that shit the previous night, within less than a day she reached out and said everything was cool and we spent the night together ... LMAO, I mean come on. So what's the moral of this story? Sadly, it is to lie. If I had just lied about the night before, everything would have been cool and we would have continued as normal, without a twenty-four hour break.

Ladies, if you find yourself in a similar situation, don't be like number six. Resist the temptation. Even if you know he is seeing other women and you think you are okay with it, eventually the feelings you develop for him will grow to excess and those other women will stop being okay. Once this happens, my suggestion would be to remove yourself from the situation.

If you finding yourself unable to let him go, then you unfortunately have to remain steadfast and comfortable with him continuing to see other women. Perhaps start seeing another guy, which may help the situation in two ways.

1. It will help you relinquish some of those strong feelings for him, as you find another man who shows you interest and who actually may care for you.

2. It may cause guy number one to get jealous and dump his other girls to be with you, which may be your end goal anyway.

To wrap the story up with number six. A few months later, the same shit happened again. We went out and she asked me why I didn't reply to some garbage message, again. I told her why, again. She flipped out, again. This time she even went to the extent of threatening me, said she would tell my parents on me or some other shit. After I laughed, I decided to end this one for good, it was just too much hassle for this type of girl. Again, if I had just lied, everything would be smooth sailing and we would probably still be seeing each other.

TREAT ME LIKE SH*T

Ladies, why do you like being treated like shit?

I mean really, what's up? I realize this goes both ways, but this predominantly affects women, and I am genuinely concerned. It's like the more we treat you like shit, the more you want us back. I guess it makes sense on some level. It's the chase; it's thrilling, exciting. A guy that shows up at your house to pick you up fifteen minutes before he's supposed to is boring, right? I mean I guess I understand. The guy who shows up an hour late without letting you know is appealing. You can spend the first half of the date fighting and then have some good makeup sex, which is always exciting.

But anyway, here is a good personal example. I was basically in love with a girl in high school that didn't give two shits about me. She was a year older than me, sexy as all hell, and had the nastiest attitude ever. She never said hi to anyone and treated everyone like shit. Somehow, it made me want her more. We were in a car together one time and it was packed. She was in the front seat, and I made a joke about her (nothing bad, just funny and with the intention to flirt) and everyone laughed. She did not laugh and instead turned around and said, "Shut the fuck up you little b*tch." I didn't speak for the next two days, yet somehow I was more in love. LOL.

On the other hand, there was this nice, intelligent, well-mannered girl who did not wear her jeans tucked into Timberland boots, and she was always interested in me. Yet I treated her as nothing more than a friend. I mean, I kept her around, but nothing past a hug-type of relationship. She even mustered up the courage one day to ask me out on a date, and I went because I was hungry, not because I liked her. I never gave her a fair shot, which is something I'll always regret because she truly was a great girl and someone who would have made a great partner.

The moral of the story here—and like I said this one goes both ways—is that we like the assholes. It is in our innate nature to be attracted to someone who isn't always there, shows up late, and is probably stepping out with someone else. But if you can somehow find your way around this love of pricks, then you may find yourself a really nice partner in life who just plain treats you well, someone you don't have to worry about each time he leaves the house, and someone you can build a great future with.

THE OFFICE

Ladies, the office is the new bar AND club. Meeting women at work has become a way of life these days. Think about it for a second, where do we spend most of our time? At work. We head off to work at 7 a.m. and don't come back until 7 p.m. We eat dinner with you, maybe go to the gym, and then by 11 p.m. or midnight we are off to bed. That is really just four hours of the day that we see you, and this is five days a week! That does not even include the work events where we get back home at 1 a.m. after saying we are going for one drink at happy hour with the team. So that being said, work is the perfect place to meet somebody. No longer does the stigma of "Don't shit where you eat" exist. People are dropping deuces all over the place in the office.

To elaborate further on this point, it's also virtually impossible to catch us doing our shenanigans at work. Especially if you work in a different field or a different location, you would never know what we are up to for those eight-plus hours a day. You may never know who we instant message on the company chat, who we grab coffee with, who we go to lunch with, who we take a walk with, who we go to drinks with, who we have dinner with, who we watch a movie with, and so on and so forth. For those eight-plus hours, we are virtually unreachable unless we want to call you back from a secret location downstairs behind the bodega and say we had meetings all day. You can't even surprise us at work because you need to have a badge to get into the building, so there goes that plan. The office has become a very discreet and effective way to generate a new relationship. We truly live in a sad, sad time.

IS THAT A NEW SUIT?

Ladies, another sure-fire sign of a man who is cheating or trying to impress someone at the office is his work attire. If he normally dresses average to work, his beard messy or unshaven, no cologne, and so on, then something is off when he takes it up a notch. If he has a sudden interest in buying a few new suits, take that as a sign that something is going on. If he starts shaving every day and putting a pile of cologne on before he leaves, take that as a sign.

You can usually tell when your man is trying to get dressed up versus when he doesn't really give a damn. So it could either be work-related, and he has a big meeting—which is probably not the case, or he is trying to impress someone at work—which is probably the case. If he is dressed up, there may be a big happy hour after work and a special someone is scheduled to be there. Or he may have a special coffee or lunch date set up with that someone.

If he is suddenly putting effort into his appearance for work, then know that something is up. There is probably someone new at work, like a consultant or an intern, or someone who has always been there but they recently connected. Either way, it's work, it's not the club, they aren't an NFL star, so they don't have to don a thousand-dollar suit to sit at a desk all day.

COFFEE

Ladies, excuse my French, but fuck coffee. If any guy at work says "Let's go grab a coffee," don't do it. This is the easiest and most unassuming way guys try to get in your pants these days. Think about it. It is the perfect cover. It's not "Let's grab drinks," which definitely has an obvious negative and a forward connotation. It's just coffee, what's the harm in a coffee, right? Wrong. It can turn into poison if you fall for it. I personally have ruined someone's life thanks to a coffee.

There was a woman at work who was in a serious relationship. Everyone was after this one, she was the cream of the office crop. And she was smart, too, not just a pretty face. The guys in the office were on it, messaging her for drinks and dinner on a daily basis. But as I said, she was smart, so she didn't fall for the bullshit traps. But I played it cool, so cool that I didn't ask her to get drinks. I didn't even ask her to go grab a coffee. I waited until I had a random run-in with her in the hallway to spark up a conversation, just said something in passing such as "Damn – nice shoes!" and nothing else.

And then I waited for the next chance encounter, and it was a Friday, so I said "What's the big plans for the weekend?" And then I still did not ask her to grab a coffee. It was on the third run-in, when we started talking for a few minutes, just casually, and then she ended the conversation by saying, "I gotta run, but let's grab coffee sometime." So I didn't even ask, and she ended up asking me to coffee (that's how the truest players work their magic, and yes, I was that good in my heyday). And then, unfortunately for her my dear readers, it was a wrap after that. A very long story short, I ruined this poor girl's life and she has been single ever since.

So don't fall for it. Don't fall for the bullshit career advice they want to give you. Don't fall for the bullshit help at work they want to assist you with. A coffee is never just coffee, it has every possible bad intention behind it.

PING: THE NEW DM

Ahh, the interoffice ping, the new way to message someone you are interested in, whose number you don't have or just want to keep restricted to a work setting. Random pings are a very easy way to hit someone up in an unassuming way. You can spark up a work topic, the weather, weekend plans, and, of course, the always-popular "Struggling today, want to go grab a cup of coffee?" Please see above. Don't fall for the coffee bs!

If you are interested in the guy and know he is single and not a founding member of the Wall Street Players Club (see below), then go for it. But odds are, he is involved with someone and has a family Christmas card being sent out at this very moment.

So, beware of the ping, please. If they want to catch up about work, set up a meeting at their desk. If they ask you to drinks, don't respond to the ping and go by their desk a little later, and say "Hey, sorry I didn't respond to your ping, I can't do drinks today," and then see how they act. See if he is looking around to see who heard that, see if little beads of sweat are starting to form on his forehead. Make him sweat, knowing that the office admin heard and will soon ask him about having drinks with a new lady at work while she is setting up a surprise baby shower for his wife.

WALL STREET PLAYERS CLUB

Beware of those charming men in senior management. These guys are the worst people in the history of people. They prey on the younger demographic of women in the office and use their work status as leverage, all to get into your pants. Meanwhile, every single one of these guys is married.

I call this the Wall Street Players Club, because I was surrounded by these kinds of men on Wall Street. The number of guys who play this game in the corporate world is astounding. From younger men to the oldest of men, it doesn't matter. Happy hours were a free for all for trying to pick up women. Maybe because this was New York City it was a bit different, but I feel like this is happening a lot these days in general, regardless of location.

But it makes sense if you think about it. These men are very successful, they are charming, they are put together in their looks, they smell good, they have money ... I mean a whole bunch of plusses. It's hard not to fall for someone like that, especially when you have a few drinks in you. But the one negative they won't say is that they are married. Every single one of them—married (or they have a girlfriend at least). Some have full-on families in the suburbs with soccer-playing and karate kids, some are newlyweds, but all of them are involved with someone.

I know it's tough not to, but don't fall for their bs. Before they lean in for a kiss at happy hour after downing a shot, think twice. Before checking into the Marriott with them, think twice. Think about that wife at home, think about the children waiting up for them to come home. And do not buy into the career bullshit, they aren't gonna help you with anything related to your career. In fact, they may do the opposite after the deed has been done and try to get you fired somehow so there is no trace back to them at work. Because imagine how will that look, if a managing director is fooling around with an intern and she throws a tantrum and e-mails someone about the relationship.

TEAM DINNER

Team dinner? No. Just stop. A team dinner, really? The only time there are team dinners is during the holiday season. The team may go out for drinks or dinner to celebrate the year, and this would only happen once. There are never multiple team dinners, companies are too cheap for that. Other than the holidays, there is no such thing. It is generally a cover up for either: happy hour with the boys, happy hour with the boys and the girls, or they are going on a date.

There is no team in corporate America that goes to team dinners every few weeks or months, because there is really no need to. Why would they, they see each other every day, LOL. Co-workers get on each other's nerves more than family does, so don't fall for the notion that they want to spend eight hours of the day with each other and then endure another two hours for dinner together, especially when they could be spending time with their own family in the comfort of their own home. Beware of excessive team outings in the evening, because they ain't what they seem!

PLEASE LET ME PLAY COD IN PEACE

Ladies – honestly speaking, we don't have much to look forward to in life, especially once we've settled down into a serious relationship. So please, if you have a good one on your hands, give us those few occasions when we are doing things that we enjoy. We are hopefully not sleeping with anyone else, we are attentive for the most part, we listen for the most part, so let us have some me time.

Fellas, if you are a good guy, you will appreciate this section. Shit, even if you are a terrible guy, you will appreciate this section. So both of you, you are welcome.

CALL OF DUTY / NBA 2K

What is it with these damn games? I have no fuckin' idea. Anytime they are on, I get into a fight with some broad. We could be having the best day of our lives, we could have won the damn lottery, and still we will get into a fight about this game. Women, you have plenty to indulge in and enjoy: shoes, bags, dresses, skirts, bracelets, rings, necklaces, and on and on. We have very limited things to indulge in compared to you.

To take it a step further, you have makeup videos, *Sex and the City*, Kardashian shows, *Dancing With The Stars*, *The Bachelor*, *The Bachelorette*, *Bachelor in Paradise*, Bachelor for Seniors, and on and on. We have one thing: a simple video game. For the love of God, let us play this game in peace. If we are playing with a friend, leave us be. If we are playing online, leave us be.

We don't bother you when you are watching your shows or online shopping or whatever it is that makes you happy. So please, we ask that you do the same for us. Have some compassion in this regard. This section is more for the brothers … just give us a little peace with this one. It goes a long way, trust me! Showing us that little bit of compassion in a video game, allowing us some time to play with our boys, it really works well with us. It shows us you care about the dumb shit we care about. I get it, it's a damn video game, it's not real. I completely understand. It's something we take seriously and gives us a little non-sexual pleasure, so indulge us, please.

FANTASY ***BALL

This is just another segue from the above, another avenue for us to enjoy a little me time. Anything fantasy is something that we love, whether it's football, basketball, baseball, whatever. We take it seriously, well, because it generally involves money and the chance to win a big pot. That should be reason enough. But aside from the monetary aspect, we get joy out of it. It's something we do with close friends, a way to keep in touch with people we don't normally talk to.

It also keeps us sharp mentally and feeds our love for sports. We have to track players and statistics and injury reports, do trades, okay this is probably getting boring for you, so I'll stop there. But just know it's something that we genuinely enjoy and take pride in, and we can actually win some money if we do it well! It's not as bad as it seems, so please let us do this in peace and have some fun. After all, we are being committed to you.

BAD GUYS FINISH FIRST

Ladies – Why do you like the worst guys possible? The bad guys really do come in first in the race, unfortunately. This is figuratively, literally, really any fuckin'-ly. This notion has always blown my mind. And I know this can go both ways for guys and girls, but it's mostly girls unfortunately. Why do you like the asshole over the nice guy? What is in you that inherently pulls you towards a guy who acts like a dick over a nice guy who is a slice of heaven. Maybe nice guys that don't cheat are boring? Maybe nice guys don't know how to handle you in the bedroom? I mean these are valid reasons, I guess, but seriously you'd rather have a cheating scumbag on your hands?

THE BEDROOM

Here is the honest, cold truth: We don't give a damn whether or not you orgasm. In fact, we prefer it if you don't so that you are horny enough to want to do it again, and then we can bust another one out. It's not a myth, this is how we think pure and simple. This is the definition of us bad guys. A good guy will hold it in, and if he comes early will service you afterward so that you can get yours. Bad dudes won't even think of that, we will either leave, go to sleep, or go eat a cheese steak.

Bad dudes have one thing in mind, that they get theirs. They don't give a damn what you do, as long as they get theirs.

POST-GASM

You can really tell a lot about a guy after sex. Actually, not even after sex, just after they have an orgasm. It may be only twenty seconds in, so it may not even count as sex just yet. But pay attention to what he does right after he pops one off.

If he is an asshole, he will act accordingly, as follows.

- He will not ask if you got yours

- He will rush to the bathroom to clean up

- He will leave within five or ten minutes by saying something came up

- He will say he's hungry so you can either cook for him or order food for him

- He will head to the club with his boys

- He will leave you butt-naked and get on his phone to text his boys or other girls

- If he cares about you, he will show it, as follows.

- He will make sure you got yours (and if not, apologize about it and say he will make it up to you)

- He will take a few seconds to step back and adore you before he gets up

- He will give you a kiss AFTERWARDS

- He will get you a glass of water

- He will ask if you're hungry

- He will order food for you or cook for you

- He will spend the night

- He will hand you your clothes and/or a robe

Post-gasm, ladies, is a surefire indication of whether he actually likes you or if he is just passing some time in his day before he gets to his night.

NOT THAT YOU

There are no stories, anecdotes, or profound convictions here. Pure and simple, here are a few signs that point to that fact that he just doesn't *really* care about you.

- He calls you "baby" only during sex

- He kisses you only during sex

- He refuses to meet your friends

- He refuses to take pictures with you

- He never meets up with you when you are out with other people

- He always uses your car when you two are going out anywhere

- He lets you pay for meals, movies, groceries, and so on

- He replies to texts from other girls right in front of you

- He asks you for rides for errands and to fix his car

- He asks you to walk his dog while he's out at happy hour

- He lets you pay for hotels for sex

You'll notice the italicized really above. It is there for a reason. He does care, a little, but not a whole lot. I mean he is still hanging out with you, listening to your stories, maintaining a good friendship, but just know that the main reason is

1. the sex

2. the meals, free rides, free errand delivery (i.e., all of the above)

NICE GUYS ... ALWAYS COME IN LAST

One of my closest buddies was a nice guy to a tee. He never had a girlfriend in elementary school or high school. He had a girlfriend in college and wanted to marry her, but she didn't so they ended things. Eventually, after college, he met a woman who was getting older, so she decided to let him marry her pretty quick. But this woman treated him like shit. She flirted with other guys, at times in front of his face. She cheated on him with old boyfriends, personal trainers, and so on. I mean she was the worst kind of partner you could imagine.

He had a golden opportunity to leave her before they got married. He found out that she was flirting with another dude that he knew, asking him to send pictures with his shirt off and saying stuff like, "I never thought you noticed me ... you are so hot..." But, my man still did not even flinch. His mind was made up that he was marrying this woman. *What can you do, right?*

He kept asking me for advice about what he should do before and even for a little while after they got hitched. I said over and over again, "End it, brother." His own brother said to end it. His family said to end it. A woman like that does not change, this behavior is deeply rooted within her. Every time she sees a good-looking man, she will wonder and possibly stray. But, my man did not listen. He was probably fearful of losing her and not having anyone else to marry. So he decided to stick it out like an idiot and basically lets her do whatever she wants.

Now, my guy has two kids with her, so he is never leaving her. She continues to do her thing on the side, comes back home, kisses her kids goodnight, and sleeps like a baby. She takes vacations with her girls all the time while my man is home with the babies. A truly lousy situation for my boy, but what else was he going to do? I guess some people would rather be pathetic and together with someone than be single and have a sense of self-respect. As long as the pictures look good on Facebook and Instagram, who cares, right?

What's the moral of this story? Nothing, really, if you were my boy, LOL. He is leading a miserable life because he was too scared to make the right decision and stand up for himself. Really, just know that you don't always have to be the nicest guy to land the girl. In actuality, if you are a bit of a dick, condescending, always late, then you will probably end up in a better relationship than if you are just nice and boring throughout. Ladies, I don't have much advice here, just enlightenment to hopefully change your views on assholes. If you want to have some fun, okay, go for the prick. But if you are looking for something serious and even marriage, just find a nice guy. Trust me, you will sleep better at night. Why? Because he will be right next to you instead of at the bar at a work happy hour at 2 a.m.

KINDLY ACCEPT YOUR ROLE

Ladies, I implore you … please try to not become a sidepiece. It is a horrible way to live. But if you do end up becoming one, knowingly or unknowingly, please try to remove yourself from the situation. If you find that you ultimately cannot, please, kindly abide by the code of being one. So again, if you are a sidepiece, I know it's tough, but be a sidepiece. If you are a main course, you may still be a sidepiece in some way. But let me start with the sidepiece …

Calling all sidepieces, we love you. Don't let anyone tell you we don't, we honestly do. You give us purpose in our lives. You bring us a level of excitement that we just don't get anywhere else. We may even be in love with some of you, believe it or not. Hell – we may even love you more than our mains, but for some reason choose not to be with you.

We look forward to texting you every morning, as soon as we get to work, which brings me to a few key sub-components of being a sidepiece and accepting your role. Sorry, this is one is going to sting, but brutal honesty may help you remove yourself from this shitty situation.

OFFICE HOURS

Like I said, we love you. You are the first person we want to talk to, after 9 a.m., and the last person we want to talk to, before 5 p.m. Please respect the office hours of this relationship as an official sidepiece. Unless you have an agreed-upon protocol with your man, I urge you not to deviate from this platform. For example, if you discuss that his main lady goes to bed by 9 p.m., then you have free reign to text after that. If the scumbag calls you every night at 11 p.m. while his wife and baby are sound asleep upstairs, then so be it. If not, please wait until the following morning (after 9 a.m., please!) to send that text. When in doubt, wait for him to hit you up first.

If, for some reason, his main lady is absent-minded or just not too bright and you can text through the day and night, then go for it. But have that conversation first and establish the clear protocol for communication.

And yes, I know, the sidepiece office hours coincide with the work day, so hopefully you are starting to see where I am going with this. As I alluded to earlier in the office sections, at work is where we do a lot of damage. This is unrestricted and private free time that we have away from you, so we can get a lot of bad shit done. This is when you will see us texting back within seconds. Because once we get home, our responses will come every thirty minutes or even hours later. So if you are a sidepiece, please respect the office hours and don't freak out if you don't hear back on a text after 5 p.m. And whatever you do, please do not call!

WEEKENDS

Under no circumstances, ever, are you to contact your man over the weekend. First, realize that he is not your man. He is somebody else's.

He is using you for one thing. Actually no, it's not just one thing, t's a few things (rides, meals, errands, etc.).

Anyway, the weekend is precious time and is reserved for the main lady and their family. Please accept this and do not text and/or call. If there's an emergency, well, there's always 9-1-1.

THE TALK

This should go without saying, as embedded in the very fabric of being a sidepiece, but I feel I must reiterate. There should never be a time when you say that you need to talk. You are a sidepiece. Your job is very simple. It is to provide the things he is not getting from his main lady:

- Sex

- Companionship

- Laughs

- And more sex (so nice I had to say it twice)

If you find yourself catching excessive feelings and want to break up his relationship and become the main, ask the man to do so. If they say no for whatever reason, then you have full reign to leave him and rid yourself of being the sidepiece. There is no obligation whatsoever for you to continue being a sidepiece. We sure as hell won't be offended. We may be upset, sure, but we won't be angry or offended. So have that conversation with yourself before having the talk, and figure out what it is you really want.

CONTACTING THE MAIN

Again, the under-no-circumstances bit applies here also. Please, under no circumstances are you to contact the main course. This, again, should go without saying, but this point also needs to be driven home. You cannot contact the main course. You will inevitably look like the idiot for doing so. If you do end up being drunk one night and contacting her, yes, you will temporarily feel better. But in the end, nothing good will come out of it for you. Again, nothing good will come of it for you.

If you do contact her, ten times out of ten the main lady will forgive the guy. I say 100 percent of the time because I am fully confident in this assertion. I have seen this firsthand many, many times with friends and family and have also experienced this myself. Once the main lady finds out, she will be upset of course. But she will give the guy a second chance. There is just too much to lose in this regard for them—social media couple pictures and stories; their friends, their family, their lifestyle. They don't want to deal with the embarrassment from friends and family over a breakup, so they will absolutely give the man that second chance. If he slips up a second time, then I have no clue, honestly. The second time really is when the main lady finds out the type of woman she is—whether she will allow this piece of shit to take advantage of her for the rest of her life, or whether she will say "Fuck what everyone thinks if I don't have a man, I'm out." This is a touchy area, I know, so I will not give my opinion here on which way to go.

FRIENDS

As difficult as this is, ladies, you should tell not your friends about being a sidepiece. It's embarrassing, first, and nothing good will come out of it. They will judge the shit out of you, tell you that you are above it, blah blah blah. Meanwhile, they are alone and unhappy as fuck. They can't even get a right swipe on Tinder, an app designed for smashing. They live sad lives and want you to be sad with them instead of having fun.

They will meddle unnecessarily and try to fuck the situation up somehow. You will probably end up fighting with them, and may even lose them as friends because of their judgment and words. So, as much as you want to, don't tell them. As long as you are happy with the situation, carry on. If you become unhappy, then feel free to leave, pass go, and collect your dignity back.

Genuine friends are great—they always have your back, come through when you need them for something, and always preserve your happiness no matter what situation you're in. The rest of your friends are jealous, vile people. They want to see you unhappy, to see you fail, essentially to see you in shittier shape than they are. That's human nature with most people, and it's just the way it is. We love gossiping about people in negativity, never positivity. When is the last time you heard your friend say, "Damn, she looks amazing right?" Nope, all you hear is "She looked awful last night, am I right? Did she really wear that ugly-ass dress? Omg, she got lipo for sure." It's sad, but unfortunately true. So do us and yourself a favor and keep the fact that you are a sidepiece to yourself.

SOCIAL MEDIA AND APPS

Ladies – Beware of social friggin' media…

IT GOES DOWN IN THE DM
(EVEN ON LINKEDIN?!)

Online dating used to be limited to eHarmony and Match. But now it has become so much more. I mean, the things I have seen lately are crazy. Guys are even cheating through LinkedIn. I mean, what the hell?! Linked-fucking-In? This is the newest trend ladies. Why? Because you would never ever think he is sliding into DMs through LinkedIn. It's a professional network, right, or it used to be.

It is sad, but true. This is actually a perfect platform to holler at girls. It is so unassuming that it actually makes it perfect to do so. You would obviously never check our LinkedIn DM's, right? Even if you saw something pop up while we were hanging out, you would assume it's work related. It's an easy cover for us to play off.

And sadly, that's not even the worst part. It's even worse for the unassuming ladies they holler at through the platform. It's going to be mostly senior, VP-level guys who prey on the innocent on LinkedIn. These gentlemen will focus on targeting mainly younger women, fresh out of college or early on in their careers who are looking for their next role at a big-name firm. They usually start by sending a connection request. Of course the young lady will not assume anything and see a senior vice president from Major Bank of Wherever sending them a request to connect, and they hit accept. That's when the first message will come, and something like this.

> SVP: "Hi Jackie! My name is Ken and I am a senior vice president at Major Bank of Wherever. I saw your profile and think you'd be a great fit for one of the roles at the bank. Would you be interested in speaking further about this?"

> Unassuming Young Lady: "Hi Ken! Of course I would love to learn more about the organization and the roles you have in mind. Can you send me a job requisition ID so I can take a closer look?"

> SVP: "Hi Jackie! Yes, I can do that [Note: He never will]. But before I do, let's chat over coffee so I can learn more about your background and see where the best fit is."

Ladies, please do not fall for this trap. It is all a plot to get some alone time with you. Coffee is never just coffee, trust me. I have done the same thing countless times. There is absolutely no reason to meet face to face in this situation. If they saw something about your profile that they liked, they can simply ask you for a resume and go from there. They can learn more about your background through a messages or, at most, a phone call. No need to meet in person, so please don't do it.

If you do, they will end up coming fully prepared. They will be wearing that shiny blue suit, the Rolex watch on the wrist, smelling like a cologne factory, polished shoes, and so on. On top of the shiny exterior, they will be charming, funny, and intelligent. This is a lethal combination, ladies, as you can probably already imagine. Senior-level folks are experts at being personable, because as part of their day-to-day jobs they have to deal with clients. Relationship management is a big part of the work environment. So they will know the right things to say to pique your interest professionally, and just the right amount of things personally to get you to let your guard down and fall for the guy. The biggest players will talk just the right amount of business to get you interested in having a second meeting. They may even say something came up suddenly during the first meeting, when it is at a good place, so you almost have to meet up again to actually talk about a specific role you want to look into.

The next time won't be coffee, either. It will be a drink. And they will pitch it so unassumingly well that it won't even seem like anything is wrong. Think about it. If he pitched you a drink on the first go-round, instead of coffee, what would you think? You would probably realize yourself that something is off. *Why does a complete stranger want to have a drink with me?* And you will likely say no or ignore their message. Rightfully so. But the real player won't ask for a drink right away. He knows that may scare you off. So he will start with a few messages, then send the coffee invitation (the best players will suggest coffee during work hours so it's even more unassuming), and when that first meeting goes all too well and he seems like a genuine guy who is interested in your career, he will end the first meeting and get your phone number, locking in that second meeting because in actuality, y'all didn't talk about anything substantial really in the first meeting.

When that text message comes in, it will sound something like this "Hey Jackie! Sorry we had to cut our coffee meeting short! I have a ton of stuff going on at work this week, so how about we meet up for a drink after work? I think I have a role that is a really great fit for you!" Again, it will sound normal. You will think, *Okay, he is busy during work hours. That makes sense because he is senior management. How much harm can one drink do at 6 p.m. He says he has a perfect role for me , so why not?* And because he was not coming on to you during that first meeting, there is no reason to think anything is wrong with this situation.

Alas, you are completely wrong. One drink is never one drink, we all know that. He might even start off with a shot to celebrate the end of a rough week or a huge presentation that he gave. And then it's a wrap, man. One shot turns into two or three, one drink turns into four or five. He will order some food, take his tie off, and charm the pants right off of you (literally). It will be an awesome night. You may not sleep with him on the first night, but you will likely make out with the guy. I mean *why not, right? He is handsome, dresses well, smells amazing, and has a great job. What more can you ask for?* Sadly, you just got duped. There will be no actual career help past this point. In fact, he will do everything he can to not bring you into his firm, because that is shitting where you eat and won't bode well for him. Think about it, why would he want the drama of a young lady coming into his firm and pretending that they are dating. So, ladies, don't fall for this trick... because it works, trust me!

FRIEND ME

Ladies, when you start seeing a guy, add him on social media fairly soon. Facebook, Instagram, and so on. You will get an immediate pulse on his family and friends. You can check to see his follower statistics, and when you see that he is following 3000 people yet has a total of two followers, you can go ahead and proceed to that handy Contact Name → Info → Block this Caller feature on your phone.

When I say fairly soon, though, don't do it on the first date, unless of course he brings it up. If he brings it up, attack right away and get in there! If not, here is what you do. By the second or third meeting, slip the social media conversation in there. "Oh I saw this really funny clip on Insta, you have to see this," or "Lebron posted something really cool on Facebook about giving his game shoes to a little girl in the stands," or any area of interest you have. And then casually slip the question in, "Oh by the way do you have Insta or Facebook?" This way it doesn't seem like you are just trying to get to his social media, but just casually asking.

If he doesn't have an Insta, or at the least a Facebook, this is a definite red flag. This is a clear indication that he is not a good dude. No matter what excuse he gives you, don't buy it. "Ah, I waste too much time on it," "Insta is annoying," nope, shut the fuck up. Insta has more hoes with their fat asses on display than porn does these days. Every guy will either have an active Insta or have a ghost account where he can just look at some quality T and A when he needs to. Seriously, if they are not willing to give up the social media, don't entertain anything long term. Trust me, you will not regret this decision.

Don't delay this social media investigation either, because this tells you right away what you are dealing with. Whether he has a main lady, kids, a crazy mother, you will come to see the type of man he really is.

HIS INSTA IS CLEAN!

Per the above, you added him and he accepted. Great! Buuuuut, even if he does add you, be careful. There are certain things he can do to still hide his dirt.

You scoured through all his pictures and there aren't any major flags. There are just tons of pictures of himself with friends, guys, girls, nothing too couple-ey. Beware, he may be telling his main lady that he is using this as a business account and it's not right to have personal relationships on there. For some damn reason, mains always tend to believe these garbage excuses LOL, so he's covered there.

You look at his stories and again, it's all good. But here is where he can hide his shit. He can block you from viewing certain stories. So while he's out with some new piece from out of town, taking pictures and posting away to increase his brand, he can simply block you from the story and you won't know anything. From your perspective, you aren't blocked from his 'gram, so everything is gravy. But for his followers and his boys, he is looking like the man with his sidepieces. If you really get serious and want some clarity, check him on this nifty little feature. Because if it looks too good to be true, then it probably is.

MARRIAGE-DATING APPS

This should be a pretty simple and straightforward concept. I mean it's 2021, and these apps have been around for a while now. But beware of these so-called marriage-dating apps. There is no such thing. Guys are just finding new and innovative ways to meet and fool women into sex.

This pertains especially to the free ones, that is, your Tinders, your Plenty of Fishes, and your OK Cupids. These are straight hookup sites. So, at least put yourself in a situation where there is an added layer, a payment. Those will weed out the especially broke and pathetic ones.

But at the end of the day, it doesn't mean much that you are on Match or eHarmony. The truest players have money, and will spend that $19.99 a month to get some ass. It is a worthwhile investment to them. Just be careful when you swipe right. Before you meet up, make him earn it. Have a few calls before you even think about meeting up. Throw a few FaceTime calls in there also (we will expand on the value of FaceTime later), which will give you a comfortable read on him.

And when you do finally say yes to meeting in person, for goodness sake don't sleep with him on the first meeting. Make him work for it. And meet at a public place. No letting him pick you up from your home. That's the worst thing you can do. He can easily come by anytime he wants when he knows where you live, door man or no door man. So meet at the restaurant. Do your due diligence before you give him the goodies.

HAVE S-E-X WITH YOUR HUSBAND!

Ladies, I want to drive this point home. Point blank. If you are married, PLEASE have sex with your husband. It sounds simple, right? It goes without saying, right? You meet a new guy, he seems nice. You go on a few dates, he's funny, pays the check. You finally decide to sleep with him, he makes you O, everything seems to be in the right place. He proposes, the wedding is great, sex life is amazing throughout. But then at about the six-month to a year mark, something happens. Not sure why this is or what triggers it, but it's like you completely lose the urge for sex.

I completely get that we are all busy people. That goes without saying. We work, go to school, have kids, basketball/soccer/karate/whatever practice, the gym, family stuff... The list goes on and on. But this shouldn't take away from that intimate time with your husband. Sex is a very important part of a marriage. I would say it's almost the cornerstone of the relationship. People will strongly disagree, and that's fine, because everyone is entitled to their opinion. I bring this point up because I want to help. I want to see fewer divorces and more old-fashioned couples growing gray together. I truly do, which is really the entire premise of this book. This brings me to some points to help.

LADIES, INITIATE!

This is very important, ladies. You have to initiate sex. If you cannot bring yourself to do it most of the time, then at least do it sometimes. That's enough! Even one out of times ... 10 percent is all we ask. We will handle the other 90 percent! I am telling you, just that one time will be enough for us, and we will handle the rest with ease.

When it comes to initiating, it just cannot always be the man. We get tired of it, both physically and then mentally at some point. Think about it. How would you feel if you had to start every time. That your husband never even looked at you in that way, never touched you, never kissed you (except to say goodnight), never grabbed you. It would suck, right? So please, if you are trying to keep your marriage strong and going, please just initiate the love-making 10 damn percent of the time.

If for some reason the setting at home isn't right, perhaps the kids are always around (which isn't really an excuse because where else would they go ... and they also go to sleep by 8 p.m.) or it's just not the right mood for some reason, then find ways around it. Initiate by finding a sitter for the kids and setting up a night out. When you get in the car after dinner, after a few drinks, bam, nail him in the backseat. If that's too much, rent a nice hotel for the evening, grab some champagne, throw on some music, and give it to him like you did when you first started dating. If you do these things just once in a while—trust me, ladies—it will mean a ton to us. We know you are busy holding the kids down, holding the house down, holding the bills down ... so just once a month even, if you show us some love, we will be good to go and stay happy (and committed)!

HALL PASS

If you cannot bring yourself to do the above, but you still want to remain married, then it's time to give your husband a hall pass. Pure and simple: Allow him to go and have sex with someone else. I am sorry if that pisses some people off, but what the hell is the point of marriage? If your own wife won't come near you other than to hand you a crying baby, then what the fuck are we even doing? I mean if you don't want to have sex with him, maybe it's time to break away. You have needs, too, so I'd rather you be happy also. But for some reason, if things are otherwise good and you want to stay together, then please give him a hall pass.

Let him freely have sex with someone, and I guarantee it will be better for both of you. He will be much more attentive when he's home, more caring, more present, probably because he feels guilty or whatever. But he will be better because he is happy now. And for yourself, maybe go out and have a fling yourself. Maybe the thought of something new will bring your drive back.

Also, if you know your man is finding happiness elsewhere, then maybe that will be the trigger you need to bring your drive back. Maybe that will push you to decide, *You know what, I have to be more aggressive if I want to make this work.* This is perhaps difficult to realize if you are just going through the motions day in and day out, but once you have that other woman in mind it may light a fire inside you and eventually get the relationship to an even better place than before. So don't be shy. Throw something nice on and get down there and do some damage! If you can't bring yourself to do so, then let the poor guy get some from somewhere.

SELF-HEALING

If you really can't get yourself to sleep with him, then for the love of Pete please don't be mad or upset when you walk in on him choking his chicken. That's another thing that also boggles my mind: that you would get pissed off about that. I mean that is the least thing possible we can do to have some fun sexually. Self-healing really helps in many ways: it reduces stress, it relieves tension, it takes our mind off of heavy things, it helps us focus (watch *Wolf of Wall Street* if you don't believe me), and, most importantly, it helps us fulfill that sexual need that we have as human beings.

It is not a form of cheating. I really hate when people say that, LOL. This is the opposite of cheating. It just helps us maintain ourselves a little bit, so we don't go out and actually cheat. Please, give us some time to work it out if you can't stand touching us with a ten-foot pole. I promise you, he will be in a better mood and you will be, too, because you didn't have to touch him!

ROAD TRIP!

Ladies – So, you are finally doing a weekend getaway with your new boo. Congratulations, that is a big step. That means he is into you enough that he is going to spend two to three days with you and you guys can really connect. Awesome! While everything seems perfect, here are some things to test and look out for. Unfortunately, if they are true, they are not good signs.

BLUETOOTH

Here we are ladies, in 2021. If the car that your man is driving doesn't have Bluetooth, then maybe you should reconsider dating him LOL. But seriously, every car now has Bluetooth capability, from the luxury to the economy. If you get in the car and see that the phone is not connected, this is an issue. There is no reason why someone wouldn't have their phone connected while driving. I mean, you can answer calls directly through the car's audio system, hands-free. You can sometimes even see text messages and respond, so why wouldn't you have your phone connected? Why? Because anytime a text or, even worse, a call comes in, we are fucked. If you see Angela calling, we are fucked. If you see John calling and we don't pick up, you will ask why we didn't pick up, and then we are fucked. So if the guy's phone doesn't automatically connect when you guys jump in the car, just ask. Play it off if you want to not come off like you are questioning him, just say, "Can we listen to that song (that you know he has on his phone)?" If he says no, well then, I don't think I have to say anything further LOL.

But if he says okay, and then goes through the process of connecting his phone again (which is a pain by the way), then ask, "Why isn't your phone already connected?" See what he says, feel it out. If it sounds genuine, great. If not, then you know what time it is.

GOOGLE MAPS

Google Maps are another good indicator for the road trip. If he rarely uses his phone for directions, and asks you to do so, that is generally an issue. You may not think twice. He is the one who is driving, so it makes sense for you to have it up and not him. But if you think about it, it is pretty easy for him to get in the car, take thirty seconds to plug in the address, and go. If he is always asking you to do so, this could be a flag.

But I would love to be wrong, so test the theory out. When he asks, say your phone is not connecting properly, so he has to use his. See his reaction. If he says, "Okay, restart your phone," or "Let me see what's going on," there is probably an issue. It would be much quicker for him to just use his and get going, so why all the interest in fixing yours to use for maps?

If he says cool and uses his, you might be fine, but maybe not. See what he does with his phone after. If he turns the volume on high and puts it back in his pocket … first, LOL. Second, that is absolute horseshit. Why would he put his phone back in his pocket if you guys are using it for directions? I will tell you why, because the phone will be on silent and no calls or texts will appear to be coming in, but the directions will still be playing loud enough to hear.

And it doesn't have to necessarily be in his pocket, either. It could be in his door pocket, or even face down in the center console, so pay attention for those things also. These are not good signs if he is doing these things. But, if he does plug the address in with no problem and then puts it face up in the middle console for you to look at anytime, you are good to go.

MUSIC

If he is always asking you to play music from your phone, this is usually a problem also. Once you see this pattern occurring a few times, try switching it up. Like I mentioned above in the Bluetooth section, just say something like, "Hey, I want to listen to that old Kanye album (that you knows he has on his phone)," and see what he says and does. Again, if he flat out says no, then I am sorry. There is nothing else to really say there. If he starts dancing around it, don't let him dance. If he says he's tired of listening to that album, push him on it, in a nice way. If he says he deleted the album, ask him why would he do that. If he says we are using my phone for the GPS, then say okay, what does that matter?

If you do get him to connect his music, then attack. Say you want to see his phone to change the track, and tell him he cannot do it because he is driving. Once your hand is on that phone, watch how he reacts. If his neck is stretching like a giraffe toward you, if he keeps looking at you, or if his hand is still on his phone while you are looking through his music [while he is driving], there is a problem. He is absolutely hiding something ladies. Time to worry, and time to take action.

CELL PHONE PLACEMENT

Another good indicator to watch out for is one that I know has been sprinkled throughout. Pay attention to where his phone his during the trip. Ask yourself if you ever see his phone during the trip. It is close quarters inside a car when you are in the passenger seat. So he will be especially careful in the car because he is driving and half of his attention will be on the road. It's a great time for a slip up.

If his phone is inside the door pocket during the entire trip and is on silent, there is a big problem. If his phone is in the side compartment on silent, big problem. If he has it in the backseat somewhere or some suitcase where he can't even see it, huge problem. So just pay attention to where that damn phone is, because I know you ladies get complacent and overlook these items when things seem to be going okay.

BATHROOM BREAKS

Another good indicator, which is elaborated on more in the chapter called Offsides—Flag On The Play, is the bathroom. If you have a six-hour road trip ahead of you, you may have to stop, what? Two or three times, maximum, right? Some people might even say two stops max.

If you see that during a six-hour trip you stopped eight times, then that's a problem. Think about it. It's completely unrestricted time to respond to texts while in the bathroom. We will say that our stomach hurts, which is causing the frequent stops and what is causing the excess amount of time in the bathroom. We can even make a quick call during the pit stop if the side is getting impatient or something comes up. There is no way for you to see what he is up to on his phone during that bathroom run. It's a great way to respond to the sidepiece, then come back to the car and start driving again. Keep an eye out for excess road trip number-two breaks!

OFFSIDES–FLAG ON THE PLAY

Ladies, here are a couple of things I've seen—and unfortunately done in the past—to hide our many indiscretions. The key to keep in mind is pattern recognition.

WHY IS THIS DUDE ALWAYS GOING TO THE BATHROOM?

After things start to get serious and you start spending more time with your man, you naturally get to know him a bit more. Their normal day-to-day habits, the little quirks they have, and, most importantly in this segment, their bowel-movement routine.

If you are hanging out consistently, you have a good grasp on his bathroom time. If you start noticing excessive time in the bathroom and he has his phone with him, that is definitely a red flag. Think about it: it's completely private, as the door will be locked. There is no way for you to see what he is up to on his phone. It's the perfect way to respond to the sidepiece, then come back to the couch and watch some more of the movie with you. In a few minutes, he can head back to the bathroom to respond again, and the cycle continues. But don't let it happen!

Call him out on it. If he says he has stomach issues, give him some Pepto to cure it. Make him take it in front of you so you know it went down. If he says no to taking it, question him on that. If he takes it like a true player, then at least you can mess with his insides for a bit.

A change in the regular patterns of his life is a clear indicator that something new is going on. If he starts doing something new or you start to see new activities or hobbies, something is probably going on.

BEWARE OF THE GYM

If your man suddenly has a newfound respect and interest for the gym, offsides, flag on the play. He is definitely either seeing someone, beginning to, or feeling someone new, and he wants to get into better shape to secure that new tail. This is a crystal-clear indication that something is popping off.

But, I will give credit where it is due. If your man was already a gym-rat when you first met him, continues to be one, and follows the same pattern throughout your relationship, then all good over here! But if there is a new and sudden interest in getting ripped, it's definitely not a good sign.

If he is starting to take protein shakes, supplements, going to GNC regularly, then yeah, something is definitely off. If is encouraging you to come with him and start working out together, that's a different story. Then I would say that he is better than most men and to never leave him, but more often than not this is not happening. The gym is actually the last place he wants you to come. Think about it. The gym is a great place to pick up a sidepiece. He can ask if she needs help on a machine. He can spark up a conversation by asking, "How many sets do you have left?" He can approach her while taking a water break. There are several ways to get a conversation flowing at the gym. Also, that is where he will look his best. While you are in the midst of working out, your muscles and physique naturally look better, veins are popping out, you've got that oily (sweaty) look going on. He will also be extra horny at the gym, too, because beautiful women are wearing the spandex, breasts are cupped in sports bra, and so on. It's like a minefield out there if you think about it. Trust me, ladies, I have done this myself. The gym is a great place to pick something up. Especially later at night when there are fewer people, and it's easier to talk to target and talk to someone when there aren't tons of people around.

Think about it also from this angle: even if he is not actively picking anyone up at the gym, he is using that time to do his dirt, for sure. Again, this is unrestricted time alone. He can respond to texts instantly, make calls, swipe right, share pictures with his boys, whatever, really. There is probably a good two-hour window of free time, when he is heading to the gym. This is a perfect time, every day, to check in with an unassuming sidepiece. He can say some bullshit to her, that after work he has dinner with his parents everyday, so she wouldn't dare bother him then. And then, right after the gym, he can check in again saying he is tired as hell, and that he has an early morning at work so he is going to bed. Bullshit, we never go to bed by 10 or 11. And he can do this every night. You will see going to the gym as a good thing. It won't seem odd that he goes every night. But just beware, this is ample time for him to do his dirt. And you can't even surprise him at the gym unless you call him to come sign you in.

I WAS WORKING LATE

This may be an obvious point, or maybe not so obvious for others, but working late is the number-one sign of an unfaithful man. Unless you have his work phone number and you call him at his desk to say hello. But even then, there is a nifty thing called call forwarding so you can redirect your office line to your cell phone. Yup, I know what you are thinking, we are really low. We can even fake a call from another number using the g-voice app. *Ahh, g-voice, you have served me well I must admit. Free does not do your services justice in the app store.* Sorry, got a little emotional there.

Working late is one of the easiest cover stories. We can say we have calls with international team members or clients. We can say we have a deadline coming up and our boss asked us to stay late. We can say we are training a new hire. We can say a bunch of shit, basically, and there is really no way for you to verify that we are lying.

But this is pure bullshit. Tell me one corporate job where you can't work late from home. Go ahead, I'll wait. You boss is asking you to work late? Okay, so come home first, then log in and work as late as you want. You have an international call? Okay, so come home and then you can take your international call from your cell phone, because any phone can dial you into a conference line. Unless you have a job where you physically have to be there to work (i.e., construction or manufacturing), you can most likely do your job from home.

So, beware of the working-late excuse, because it is usually complete bullshit. It is generally a cover story to attend happy hour with the boys, go on a date with someone new, or kick it with a sidepiece.

I HAVE A CONFERENCE OUT OF TOWN

If your man pops up out of nowhere with a conference or a training, be the-fuck ware. Let me tell you a little something about work conferences. They don't come up out of nowhere. They take months of planning, months of preparation, and rarely is there ever an immediate need to go out of town.

Again, he can show you all the proof you want. He can create fake hotel confirmations, he can create fake e-mails from work showing conference details. We can do so many things with technology these days it is nutty. The biggest players do this even before you ask to put your mind completely at ease. They will have an-email up at home and, while you are walking by, say something like "Man, I don't want to stay at the Hilton again. That place sucks." just to get you to take a quick look and have a laugh together about it. Poor, unknowing you might think, *Okay, he just showed me the confirmation without even me asking, I have a good man.* Sorry, babe, you may have a good man, but he is a better player.

Conferences are a phenomenal cover up. It gives your man completely free reign for a few days to do whatever he wants. The wedding ring will be locked in the safe on check-in, and he is good to go. He can take a trip with his boys to Miami or Vegas for a few days of picking up women and strip clubs, or, even worse, he can take a trip with a side-piece. Since he is at a conference, he will be busy a lot with trainings during the work day, and then work dinners with the team at night. I don't want to hear shit about that. During a work dinner, he can always pick up your call. Maybe during the day he can get away with it, but at night, no. He can always step away from dinner or drinks to pick up his wife's call. There is never a time when he cannot. No team member or boss would ever look down on that.

Don't get lazy when your man has an out-of-town conference and everything seems to be fine. Do your homework, get the exact hotel name, address, and phone number. Get his schedule during the day and after work. Find out when he was team events at night and when he has free nights. If he is calling you around 9 p.m. to say goodnight and he is tired, fuck that bullshit. Wait twenty minutes, and then call back. If he answers, great. But he won't … he will likely be on the way to the bar or out with the sidepiece. Call his cell again in five minutes, and then go in for the kill. Call the hotel directly and ask to be put through to his room. I guarantee you, no one will pick up. This won't be possible. There is zero chance that he does not hear a hotel phone ringing, those things are loud as hell. He could always say he had his ringer on silent on his cell, which is believable, but the hotel landline, no way. If he doesn't answer that hotel phone after saying he is going to sleep thirty minutes ago, you know something is up.

If he doesn't answer, get that fool sweating. Send him a text saying you called the room and no one answered. I guarantee you he will be a puddle at that point. He is probably far away from his room, so it will take time to get back, and he won't want to mess up whatever he has going on at present, either. See how he reacts. He knows the hotel phone thing is hard to dodge, so likely he will rush back to the room and pretend he was in deep sleep. If there is still no response, maybe he thinks he can say the ringer was off in the hotel room or that the phone wasn't working.

At that point, if you really want to know where he is, or to just fuck with him, send him another text saying you are worried and that you are going to ask that someone from the hotel to go check on him to make sure he is okay. I guarantee you, a call will be coming in shortly. Mostly likely from his cell phone saying he was sleeping, but do not buy that shit. Say you called his room and there is no answer. Don't let him slide on his bullshit, call him out with specifics and demand answers.

WHO WAS AT THE DOOR?

If you are hanging with your man at his crib and he has a rotation going on, it's likely that one of the other ones may just show up one day. Especially the crazier ones—smh—the crazy ones. If someone ever rings the bell or knocks on the door while you are chilling and he does not answer, red flag. Why wouldn't he answer his door? If he looks through the peephole and says it's a salesman or FedEx, go check it out for yourself. Never just trust what he is saying. Always go and look.

This happened to me one night. I was chillin' in the kitchen with one of the girls, making dinner for her and drinking some wine. It was starting off to look like a great night, and then bam, or ding I should say. My worst nightmare. I went to the door and looked through the peephole, and I saw another sidepiece, the craziest one of them all. *Fuck.* I mean, who else would show up unannounced but the crazy one.

I, of course, was panicking, but kept my cool. Because that is the golden key when it comes to being a player: keeping your cool in all situations. I played it off right away, said it was one my roommate's crazy girlfriends when it was really mine. Out of the kindness of her heart, she believed me and we continued cooking dinner.

A minute later, ding. I couldn't believe it. This crazy girl rang the bell four times. I mean, *what the hell, four times?* Suspicion started to build a little bit. She asked why not just open the door and tell her he isn't home? I had to take it a step further. Again, very coolly, I said that my roommate told me specifically, "Don't answer the door for her." "She would come in and never leave and start breaking shit." She looked at me funny for a second, but bless her heart, she said, "Okay. Well, then, we wouldn't want that." Still panicked that she was still there and wouldn't leave, I made up some bullshit to leave from the back of the house, just to get away from the possibility that she may still be there lingering out front. I don't even know what I said to make it justifiable to leave from the back of the house, through the backyard, LOL, but it worked. We left and went to go grab a couple of drinks and caught a flick, waited long enough for it to be well into the night... and then came back home. Just to be on the safe side again, I parked behind the house in the parking area for the next set of townhouses and we walked the quarter mile back to the house. To cover it up, I said I parked there because my roommate's mom was coming early the next morning and I wanted to give her the parking spot. She said, "Aww, that's sweet of you," and thought nothing else of it. I mean, *Come on, girls, let's be smarter in these situations. Pick up on the signs of the BS!*

All in all, if she had just made the decision to open the door, or make me open it in front of her, I would have been screwed. The women would have met each other, and my rotation would have gone down by two. When in doubt, just answer that damn door.

GULP

Okay, so you found something out about your man that is not good, and you want to verify whether or not it is true. After you ask him, pay attention to what he does next and his body language. Here are a bunch of things to look for and the tell-tale signs that he is hiding something.

You: "I just got a message from someone named Claudia Who's that?"

- Him: "What do you mean, who is that?"

  · It's a simple question, you clown. Who is this girl that is messaging me about you?

- Him: He may pretend like he didn't hear you and ask, "What did you say?"

  · You are a foot away, how can he not hear you all of a sudden LOL. Plus, he heard when you asked him what he wanted to eat when he was in the other room.

- Him: "I just woke up and already with this shit?"

- Yes, important matters need to be discussed right away. Because you are just waking up, you think I should wait until what, dinner, to ask you something important?

If he cannot answer you right away saying that he does not know who that is, firmly, then you have a problem. If he starts stuttering, then you have a problem. If he starts to sway around, then you have a problem. If he gets mad and storms out abruptly, saying some bullshit like, "I am so tired of this," then you have a problem. If he truly has nothing to hide, he will clearly and firmly say to your face that he has no idea who the girl is or that she is lying and will address the situation head on. If he squirms, he's cheating.

Here is another insider tip: look for the gulp. This is a sure sign when someone gets nervous after being asked a question. It's especially noticeable on guys, too, because of the Adam's apple. If you ask him a question about another possible woman in his life, or anything really that he is hiding, look for the gulp. For me, personally, as soon as I got asked a question like that my throat instantly (and I mean instantaneously, that split second) dried up like a clam. It was a psychological response for me, because every time I heard one of those questions my body reacted that way without fail. And then, as you all know, when the throat is dry we naturally take a gulp to get some water back into the well. So, pay very close attention because this is hard to see if you are not looking for it. Right after you ask the question, take a look at the throat area and look for a gulp. If he gulps, he's lying. Also, if, while you are asking him about a particular woman or the events of a particular night out, he reaches for a drink all of a sudden, you know what's up. He is preemptively trying to water the well so that he is ready to dish out five minutes of pure bullshit.

Another insider: sweat on the forehead. If you see tiny beads of sweat starting to form on his forehead and he is looking extra shiny all of a sudden, then you know he is nervous and probably has something he's hiding. But if he is cool as a cucumber when you are asking him about some serious allegations, and even goes the extra step to prove it somehow, then you can relax. He's a good dude. Unless he's a serial killer, also because those mothafuckas are stone cold and can even pass a polygraph. If that's the case, then, again, you have an entirely different problem on your hands.

GETTING PULLED OVER

This is a great little tidbit. First, when we leave to do something by ourselves, in our own car, this is like heaven to us. This is one of the most gratifying things in the world when in a relationship. It is unrestricted, free time for us to call whoever, text whoever, and go wherever. So if it takes two hours to grab a carton of milk from the store down the block, then yeah, something's afoot. But here is a great one that I have done countless times, and it works like a charm.

When I was heading somewhere, on perhaps a longer trip, usually I was up to no good on the way. Stopping by and seeing old girlfriends, sidepieces, it was always fun. Usually with a main, she is on it. She calls every few minutes to check in, wants to talk while I am driving. Because why not? I mean if a guy is just driving, why wouldn't he want to talk to his lady the whole time, right? And unfortunately, we can no longer use the "Let me drive, I don't want to get pulled over," excuse anymore. Because every car now comes with Bluetooth and we are hands-free, so there goes that.

So I thought long and hard, *What can I do to get a damn half hour to hour of uninterrupted time so I can pop one off?* So what did I do – being the noble guy I am, I tried a long shot. I said "Shit, let me go, I'm getting pulled over." This worked like a charm. No calls came in, only texts asking if everything was okay. They know if we are talking to the cops and he sees several calls coming in, he will only assume that his assumptions of you talking on the phone while driving were cor-rect. I've used this several times anywhere from a half-hour car thing to once a two-hour hotel rendezvous. And they would never question it. I said, "Yeah I was being questioned. What did you want me to do? Yeah they are searching my car. What did you want me to do?" And it's all about attitude and how we sell it. If we act pissed off and/or scared, it only makes the story sweeter and more believable. So, beware ladies, if your man seems to get pulled over a lot on his road trips, there is something definitely wrong and you can assume he is using that unre-stricted free time for no good.

HAIL MARY

Ladies – I want to end this book with a section on the coveted Hail Mary. Though this term can have a few different interpretations up to the holiest of prayers, I am going to bring it down to good old-fashioned American Football—the sport that has the Super Bowl, Rose Bowl, NFL, Tom Brady, and so on.

A brief explanation for my non-football readers. Imagine two teams are playing in the Super Bowl. There are ten seconds left in the game. One team is down by four points, so they can't go for the three-point field goal to win or even tie the game. They are in enemy territory almost sixty yards away from the end zone to score. They have time for one, final play. This is the Hail Mary, which essentially refers to the last resort, the final shot, the last chance for victory. The teams form on both sides, the ball snaps into play, and the quarterback launches that sixty-plus-yard pass into the end zone for glory.

Ladies, if you have tried to flesh out whether or not you have a good man on your hands through any or some of the above sections and he checks out or somehow maneuvers out of the situation, then it's time for the Hail Mary. First, I am sorry if these scenarios have not helped to enlighten you about your man or if they pure and simple have not been effective in detection. When all else has failed and all other options have been exhausted, here are a few things you can do to get that final touchdown.

FACETIME

This feature has revolutionized the player's game, in a horrific way. All of our tricks and acts of fuckery, such as:

- While on a date with a sidepiece, going to the bathroom to call the main lady and say you are going to bed soon

- Replying to texts from the main lady while sitting across the booth from the sidepiece, so she has no idea who we are texting and we are saying it's one of our boys

- Steve from work texting in front of you and him letting you see the name so everything is all good

All of that bullshit goes down the drain when a damn FaceTime call comes in. Luckily, I was smart enough to anticipate these issues when FaceTime first came out. The idea was cool, but I didn't touch that shit with a ten-foot pole. I knew the implications that would arise with this technology, so I never hopped on the trend. Every time one of the rotation would try to bring this into the relationship, I shut it down. I never picked up any FaceTime calls and just called back normally and said, "What was that? Oh FaceTime. Man, fuck that shit. That shit is weird." Shutting it down early is very effective I must say. Because once you start, you won't be able to stop it from happening. And as soon as you stop using it, they will get suspicious. *Wait what I am doing – this is a tip for the guys isn't it? Hmmm … next book idea?* Haha, I am kidding. I am done with that part of my life and I am proud of it. I will never go back.

So, as I was saying, there is no bullshitting a FaceTime call. To counterbalance the above bullshit tactics, here are some suggestions about what to do.

- While on a date with a sidepiece, go to the bathroom to call the main lady and say you are going to bed soon:

  - Counter: On FaceTime, the main will see they are in a bathroom, not getting ready for bed. Oh and that they are dressed up and their hair is done.

- Replying to texts from the main lady while sitting across the booth so you have no idea who we are texting and we are saying it's "ne of our boys:

  - Counter: The main will see that you are in a restaurant, and even if we said we are with the boys, all she has to do is ask us to turn the phone around and see who we are really with.

- Steve from work texting in front of you and him letting you see the name so everything is all good:

  - Counter: Once you answer that FaceTime call, it won't be Steve on the screen. It will be another woman.

SEND ME A PICTURE OF YOU AND JOE

Whenever your boo says he is going to hang out with the guys or go chill with his friend, it's simple. Get proof. This is the simplest yet most effective thing you can do to make sure he is where he says he is. First, before you ask, build the rapport. Text with him a few times back and forth, ask him how Joe is doing ... ask where they are ... whatever you normally talk about. A true connoisseur knows that a few texts to the missus will go a long way in keeping her mind at ease.

But after a few texts back and forth, drop the picture line and see what happens. Just casually work it in if it's not a norm to ask. Just say, "Hey I haven't seen Joe in a while, take a picture of you guys." A picture should take, what, four seconds to take? So if you don't hear back right away, you know something is up, especially if you've build that rapport and have been texting back and forth. If all of a sudden he stops responding, you know what's up. He's not with Joe.

He will likely do a few things here:

1. He may stall, saying Joe went to the bathroom, but that will only buy him a few minutes at best and he will still have to come up with a picture to send you.

2. He may send you an old picture of him and Joe, but since you know what he was wearing when he left it will be hard to pass that one off.

3. He may, and here's the most devious one, crop a picture in with Joe really quick. But you can detect this if he sucks at Photoshop and, again, the timing. If the picture comes an hour later, you know something is up.

4. And my personal favorite, which I can personally attest has worked on several occasions, he will say that Joe had an emergency come up and had to leave abruptly. This is a perfect out for the picture. The truest of players will even call you to tell you the story to sell it even better because, as we all know, ladies love it and feel better when we call instead of a text. At that point, he can

say he's heading back, take another half hour with his sidepiece and close the evening out with her, then head back home to you.

But if he sends you the pic right away, you know he's good to go (at least that time anyway). If not, he is unfortunately doing something he doesn't want you to know about. And it's likely another woman.

AAA (EMERGENCY ROADSIDE ASSISTANCE)

I actually came up with this plan for one of my close buddies. He was going through some sh*t with his to-be wife. We met up for drinks and he broke it down. He knew his fiancé was always a big flirt, which was fine with him. But he needed to know that she wasn't crossing the line into stepping out on him. He was desperately trying to find a way to validate this. He did catch a break one day when she left her phone in his car and then went back to her house.

Everyone has a password on their phone, right? Of course, but luckily he caught two breaks that day. While they were walking together after dinner back to their car, she opened her phone to read a text message and he caught her code out of the corner of his eye. After thinking about it for a few minutes, he decided he needed to know. He entered in the code, unlocked the phone, and unfortunately saw a few things that were not copasetic.

She was still talking to her ex-boyfriend. The conversation was mostly about them both missing each other and him asking her to meet up (although it did not appear as if she actually took him up on the offer). He also saw her flirting with a guy that her fiancé knew. He was a little older and they weren't the best of friends, but this guy was widely known throughout the community and was a handsome dude. He was sending her pictures of him on vacation in his beach gear, and let's just say she wasn't telling him to stop. The next time they met up, he gave the phone back, and questioned her on what he found. She was dumbfounded to say the least, and had no clue he was able to crack her code and get into her phone. She really had no argument except to say that she was just flirting, not acting on anything, which by the messages appeared true. Now my buddy, bless his heart, is a bit aloof when it comes to these things, and a bit of a p**sy to make things worse. So he let it go and things went back to normal. Another few weeks went by and he called me, as it was getting close to the big day. He was going crazy and needed to know if she was doing the same shit behind his back, or even worse this time, and was desperate to find out the truth. He wanted to make a decision before the day of the wedding, and vowed that he would call it off if he saw anything out of whack. Enter myself. I already had been thinking about his situation and came up with a plan. For this to work, it has to be executed quite carefully, so here we go…

This is the exact plan I came up with for my buddy, but I will lay it out from a woman's perspective for purposes of this book.

Plan a dinner a few weeks in advance. Make a reservation at a nice and comfortable place, preferably a restaurant that you both have been to a bunch of times, so there is nothing out of the ordinary and your man thinks it's just another Friday night. The night before the dinner date, don't charge your phone. By the time you're ready to leave for dinner, have your battery drained as much as possible, preferably between the 5 and 20 percent range. You will need some juice, as you will need to have your phone on and ringing a little later in the evening.

On the way to dinner, casually slip in that you forgot to charge your phone all day and that your battery is almost dead. He won't think twice about it, it's just another day of you being on your phone all day on Instagram and not charging your phone. When you get to dinner, act casual, calm, and collected. Order the usual food, grab a few drinks, enjoy your appetizers. Right before the entrees come out, it's show time. I would say choose this timeslot because you guys have to eat entrees, there's no way around that. If you wait until dessert, you run the risk of him saying he's not in the mood and wants to just go. So go for the entrée.

Prep your girlfriend before the dinner so she knows the deal and just how important timing is. Choose someone reliable because this is a big night. It will probably make or break the relationship. Also, before date night starts, change the name of your girlfriend in your phone to your dad and memorize her number!

Keep your phone on the table and visible to your man. Right after the appetizers are finished, text your reliable girlfriend saying to call you in exactly five minutes. Continue the conversation as normal so, again, nothing seems out of the ordinary. When the phone rings, make sure it's loud enough so he hears it and takes notice that it is your dad calling. Start the covert conversation with "Hey dad" or however you normally greet him. And then after about thirty seconds or so, say "Dad, I can't hear you." In that time, turn your phone off using the side lock button. If you have an iPhone (sorry for people who don't, you will just need to adjust the plan a little to shut down your phone manually), just hold the button down for about three to four seconds while you are on the phone. Then, when it seems like the call was cut off, you bring the phone down to look at the screen and swipe the "slide to power off" to the right so the phone shuts down. Give it a few random taps to pretend like you are fidgeting with it. Then flip it around to show him the screen, press the home button a few times and also the lock button to show that the battery is dead. Then, somewhat nervously, state "My dad sounded like he needed something … shit … hey, let me get your phone and call him." If he says, "Oh wow no problem, here you go, babe," ladies, I applaud you. You have a wonderful man and should feel very lucky and blessed. I am truly proud!

But, if the response takes a different trajectory, then Houston … we have a fuck*n problem. If he flat out says, "No, oh hell no, it's a wrap," run and done. But odds are he's not a complete asshole and he will say yes. Have you ever seen a fish squirming out of water? Well, you're about to! I guarantee this will be the most focused you've ever seen your man on you, while you have his unlocked phone in your hand. From his perspective, he will hope that after he unlocks the phone and brings you to the call screen, that all you will do is call and sit there at the table so he can watch your every move and make sure not another screen is accessed. So, call the call same girlfriend from his phone and begin the conversation. After a few seconds, say "Dad, I can't hear you … Dad? … Can you speak up?" and then swiftly get up and quietly motion to your man that you are going to go outside really quick and be right back. Book it directly to the front of restaurant and, when you get outside, run (don't walk, in case he is a few steps behind you) to the nearest hiding spot. Important: While you are getting to your spot, make sure you keep your girlfriend on the phone live so that the phone does not lock! When you get to your place of hiding (around the building, in between cars, etc.), go for it, up to a fifteen-minute window. If you go beyond fifteen minutes, you risk your man having an aneurysm or calling 911). Check all of the major outlets first, text messages, WhatsApp messages (because as stated earlier these can be hidden very easily), camera roll, phone call log, e-mail (make sure to check the sent box also). If you still have some time after going through the core items, swipe through the phone screens to see if there are any red-flag apps (Tinder, Google Voice, etc.). Also, check his social media apps to see if there are secondary accounts you don't know about and check the private messages and DMs. If you see stuff you want to bring up later, take screenshots and send them to yourself via WhatsApp, as text messages will be harder to delete without deleting the whole trail. Odds are you guys don't communicate regularly through WhatsApp, but make sure to delete the WhatsApp message and don't forget to delete the screenshots from the camera roll and to empty any deleted items in the camera folder.! By now, you should have a solid picture of what he's up to, so head back inside. Pretend that nothing out of the ordinary happened, make up a story about Dad, and continue the evening.

When you get home, take a moment to process everything. Ask yourself a few questions.

- How many red-flag apps (Google Voice, Tinder, Go SMS Pro, etc.) did you find?

- How many women are in the picture?

- What were the messages like to each?

- What did his camera roll consist of?

- How were the DMs looking?

- Who were his recent calls to?

Unless he's super careful and deleted everything before your outing, you now hopefully have some solid intel for the first time. If you kept the evening familiar (hopefully picking a usual restaurant, go-to dishes, etc.), then the likelihood of him deleting everything is actually really low (we get lazy, especially if you ladies don't ever have access to our phones).

Now, ladies, given all of this information that you just learned, the next move is up to you. But I do want to help, my goal is to inform and advise. Not only do I want to inform you of the devious tricks of men, but I also want to provide an opinion, because I do care, and I truly do want to help. So, if I see something outlandish I will have definitely voiced my opinion and urged you strongly to leave. If it's a workable situation, I will likely have said to stay (no one is perfect, especially us guys). And finally, if you have thrown the Hail Mary and he comes out clean, catch that pass ladies. Score the touchdown. He is a wonderful man, a true keeper, do not let him go! ☺

CLOSING HOPE

Ladies – Thank you so much for taking the time out of your day to read through this. I truly hope this had shed some light into the dark world of us men, and the lengths we go to, to be promiscuous and unfaithful. My hope is that if you are able to find a few or more of the flags outlined in this book, you will simply walk away. Let him go, leave the situation, and try to find someone better. Because as the old saying goes, once a piece of shit, always a piece of shit.

Til next time!